Explosive

Eargasms

A Collection of Poetry by

Professor Julius Noble

Glover Lane Press
Publishers Since January 2000
4570 Van Nuys Blvd Suite 573
Sherman Oaks, CA 91403
gloverlanepress@gmail.com
www.gloverlanepress.webs.com

Explosive Eargasms by Professor Julius Noble
Category: Poetry
MCN: CFJ5F-BXJDB-0KQ4K
© copyright 2012-11-30 18:26:11 - All Rights Reserved

Writers Guild Registration #7246531

Cover Design: Azaan Kamau
Interior Image Provided by The Noble Trinity Corporation

ISBN 0-9789869-4-6   **(Noble Trinity Corporation)**

4

Dedications & Acknowledgements

Explosive Eargasms is dedicated to the loving memory
of my grandmother.

To my sister Pepper for her unwavering love and
support

To Ifalade for her creative inspiration

To my life partner for her love and always having a
brotha's back

To my descendants for being keepers of the legacy

To the book stores, radio stations, colleges and cultural
organizations that support my work all year long.

To my Detroit fam, we #1!

And last but not least, to my fans. I do what I do for
you...

P.J. Noble

6

Introduction

Explosive Eargasms is a collection of poetry by Professor Julius Noble expressing his journey as a young African-American male to becoming an adult in the gritty streets of Detroit. The love, pain, creativity, lessons—all move through the words and sentences on these pages. Readers will experience a frank, real, sometimes brutal view of the author's life journey. They will also understand the courage and tenacity it has taken for him to survive all that he's survived to pen this first book of poetry. Look forward to many more books to come, as well as the musical accompaniment to the written outline of a Black man who refused to let life defeat him. On behalf of *Noble Trinity Publishing* and *Glover Lane Press*, we give you, *Explosive Eargasms*. Ase....

Noble Trinity Corporation
Where the Phoenix Continues to Rise

Explosive Eargasms

Table of Contents

Birth of a Man

Like a hunchback in the primitive stages of life…

I stand in the rain
Anger and pain trapped in my mind and heart
It has not appeared on my face yet
I began to roam
The rain continues to pour
Tears roll down my face
Because I can't contain them anymore
As I drift through the urban mist
Clenching my fist
On the edge of life
In transition
From Nigga To Man
While howling up at the moon
I heard the transcendent message from the voice of Christ
My inner core became warm
The brisk air whistled a melody
Then with a booming crash, a sudden blaze brightened the
sky
Drying my eyes
A gentler breeze presented comfort and ease as I chanted
this prayer

God Wing My Mystic Flight Through Future Worlds

Where dreams cannot picture
I am perfectly made in your image
Though not with my daily actions in this Spiritual War
I leave home to die or to deliver my higher power
And free my ancestors from bondage…

After Work (For D)

Office politics
I know it can be stressful
They won't leave alone
You can lose yourself when there is no balance
Let me pamper you
Remind you
That you are a woman and not a robot
Let me pamper you, remind you
With a hot bubble bath, exotic candles burning
Sade singing in the background
Let me massage your feet
Work my way up your spine
Like the itsy bitsy spider with my tongue
You inhale and let the tensions escape
Through every moan and with every stroke
From every kiss
If we don't take time for us
We will lose our love
Let's make love off our natural buzz
Climaxing together
I'm in the mood for love and war
Under the influence
Let's work up an appetite then dine at Bennihana's
I promise to send you to work satisfied with a smile
So that you won't get lost masquerading up in that office....

Missing You

I do miss you
I miss us and our passionate history
Last time I saw you my mask was so cold and distant
I pretended what we had was meaningless
Because I knew that would hurt you

The truth is, it only hurt me more
You looked so good
I just wanted to grab you and kiss you
Fall to my knees and beg you to come back home
Instead I froze
Ignoring you as you spoke to me
I don't know how I can act so silly and childish
But I do and I did
The last time I saw you
I had to get alone and write down how I truly feel
I know you know me better than that
I hope you see through my nigga act
I am starting to see
That may be part of the reason you left
At times I can't stand my fucking self
If I ever see you again
I swear, I would do better
They say you don't miss what you have
Until it's gone
Baby come home!
Baby come back to my arms!
Let's make love stronger than we ever have before
I am willing to change
Only if you help me transform
Into the man you need me to be
I miss us…

Us and Ours

My love
Don't fail me now
During these trying times
The world is cold enough
I need you by my side as an ally
Not an enemy
I need you to be my friend
Make love to me like I'm your husband
If nothing else, I need you to be for real
I am as real as real can get
I am committed to success
Whatever it takes to obtain it
For us and ours
Don't fall apart on me now
Times are hard but your man is here
Talk to me about us and ours and how
We can make it last forever
I am listening and willing
And very capable
I love us

Miss Lovely

Dear Miss Lovely
Beauty of Innocence
Her hair is long, beautiful and dark
Holding the morals and mannerisms of my ideal princess

Dear Miss Lovely
Beauty of Innocence
Though her lips are voiceless
Her expressive silence reveals
Her erotic savageness swelling
Deep within the gates of her virgin senses

Dear Miss Lovely
Beauty of Innocence
Her captivating appearance is sharing a resemblance of an
old childhood love
My ideal princess
Making tonight sleepless
As I struggle to fight unfulfilled fantasies of her and I
making love
During this winter storm by candlelight

Dear Miss Lovely
Beauty of Innocence
My secret taste and desire for romance are rapidly
enhanced
From the mere thought of your form
Yet I patiently await my chance
To feel your lips quivering against mine
As we make love during this savage storm

Dear Miss Lovely
Beauty of Innocence
My nights remain sleepless
The need remains unfulfilled
However I still deeply admire your beauty
When I look deep into your eyes
I do see a gleam of innocence
Ohhh the beauty of innocence
Oh how I want to explore the depths
Of your sensuality and tenderness
The pleasing pain and the viciousness
Where others cannot, I will
Attend to your exotic needs with obedience
My Dear Miss Lovely, Beauty of Innocence....

Master Key

(Master key is an erotic poem of unrestricted passion)

Would you be surprised?
If I told you that I think about you more than often
Or that I have fantasized being inside of you
Exploring the deepest, darkest side of you
That has not yet been discovered
Would you be enlightened to learn?
That another woman exists inside of you
Yearning to be liberated
But kept a prisoner
Hidden away like some dirty, nasty secret

I have the master key
To unlock, open and free her
I have the nutrition to feed her
A fountain to quench her insatiable thirst
If only she had the courage to take the first step
Or do we continue to pretend that she does not exist?
From when our eyes first met to our first kiss
You act as if you are ashamed of how wet you get
Yet you still flirt
Let her go!
Before I take her from the secret garden
Ravish her in the jungle
Like the lion taking whatever he wants
Like a savage beast who ain't ate in weeks
He selfishly eats
You couldn't come on your own
So I had to use my Master Key to set you free
How does it feel to be an escaped prisoner?

Made to come against your will
A raging river spills from your body involuntarily
Guilty pleasures got the pretty redbone blushing
Masterful strokes keep the pretty redbone coming
Gushing high tides like the ocean
Crashing against a towering mountain out in sunny
California
Animals strike curious poses
Because they are wondering
Will there be any leftovers
After the King of the jungle has finished

Fall No More

Fall no more is a very special piece to me. We fall down but we get up.
Spirit moved me and Fall No More was born. P.J. Noble

I find myself restarting and reinventing myself
Repeatedly activated by the blood sizzling through my
veins
Fall no more!
I chanted this concept into a character
And became its first faithful disciple
Mentally elevating myself to a higher level
Strategically maneuvering across these plantations
Brokenness used to bring forth depression
But now it only activates this barbaric intellectual
Challenging me to illustrate these emotions with words
Constructed to produce visuals
Vividly painting a perfect picture
Of this filthy, blood thirsty, manipulating society
Which calls me anti-social and my thinking corrupted
Or corrupting
Hazardous to your impressionable public
Targeted by soul assassins
While I'm merely a reflection
A mirror-splitting image of a God-fearing, hypocritical,
cold-calculating predator
Subject to commit murder
To enforce the law and the constitution of Grand Royal
Corporation
The organization conspiring revolution
With right away action
Founded by Professor Julius Noble...

Love Drug

I can't sleep
Staring up at the ceiling fan spinning
Silence has never been so loud and distracting
This bed has never seemed so enormous
I keep tossing and turning
I feel incomplete without you here next to me
The sweet taste of your love on my tongue
Baby, your love is my drug of choice
Getting me higher than I've ever been
As I lay here lifeless, sweating and yearning
With my body craving your body like an addict
In remembrance of our last embrace
How luscious your lips felt
As I held you in my arms
I remember feeling how small the world seems when we
are together
Baby, your love is my drug of choice
I feel sick when I don't get a fix
I can't sleep
I can't work
I need my *night nurse* to stop the pain from getting any
worse
With your special therapy, your healing hands massage my
soul
Baby, your love is my drug of choice...

Awakened

Too many unanswered questions
From a man with no identity
Soul searching
Finding myself lonely and hurt
Surrounded and outnumbered
Drowning, swept away by the current
As the world turns, sex, drugs and money dictates
My heart aches when I reflect
Hindsight is always 20/20
I regret so many errors
I wasted too many years suppressing my talent
Now the sleeping has awakened
Asking my God how much more must I endure before I
break?
Lord knows, I am a product of my environment
Trying to elevate my consciousness
Michael threw the devil out the gates of heaven
Julius Noble, the Guardian Angel of the Ghetto
Here I stand before you, no gimmicks
Voted in by my constituents to awaken the people
I am the unheard voice of the struggle
I am my brother's keeper
I am no longer sleeping….

I Hurt Too

At times I want to scream at the top of my lungs
Nearly brought to tears from the pain I feel
Yet, my super, macho ego won't allow me to submit or
break
I sob internally and abuse my body
By overdrinking and over-smoking
Instead of the pain, my strength escapes
I isolate myself to regain my composure and focus
Wholeheartedly on this battle zone which has no mercy
It's not easy being a nigga
But I really wouldn't expect you to understand the product
of this battlefield
Under constant attack and space invasion
Mentally collapsing from internal disasters
My exhausted soul craves your sweetness and tenderness
Only with you can I lower my defenses
Bathing in your internal river
Sensuous woman who understands
Taking my rage and stripping it down to raw passion
Saturating the sheets with a splash
As we bathe together
Recapturing the magic during the truest moment, in my
purest form
Your body quivers as it absorbs my love
Delivered with vigorous energy
Renewed by you, sensuous woman

Toxic Love

I can't get you out of my system
You love is like a drug
I am addicted to it
When I try to walk away
When I think I'm over you
I get pulled right back in
Your beauty can make a Preacher Man sin
Your loving is like kryptonite to a demon
Eve had Adam eat that apple because Adam was not strong
enough to lead her
Give me back my rib
The wisdom of Solomon
My God, I beg of you
I don't want to be another weak fool
God has made you for me so that I would not be alone
laboring for Him
What would make you think that you are smarter and
stronger than the both of us?
It must be the devil
Don't let him in
Don't make me choose between you and our Benevolent
creator or my service to Him
I need a good woman, partner and helper to help me
Together we can raise a nation that will praise His name
and imitate His loving way....

Royal Court

Who are you?
Friend or Foe
Praying for my downfall
No weapon formed against me shall prosper
I am a Prophet of Truth
Warrior for freedom
Champion, lover, King of the Jungle
Professor Julius Noble
Who are you?
Friend or Foe?
Speak now!
Stake ya' claim now or get from around these parts
I swear
In the name of my Creator
From this day forward everything artificial around me shall
perish
Within twenty four hours, wrath is coming to restore proper
order
Who feels it, knows it
You are guilty until proven innocent
You are broke and can't afford love
So you hate, murder and burglarize
Ain't nobody killing us but us
I'm not going to touch you but you must learn
From this day forward your decisions will haunt you
Who are you?
Friend or foe?
Dark secrets brought to light examined closely

Facts determine if you are worthy to sit at the table among bosses
Who are you is the question
Only you know in your heart of hearts the answer
Real G's stay ruthless taking secrets to the grave
As head of my family, with all the powers invested in me
I order the heads of all imposters on the mantle by the morning
Conference is adjourned
Back to the Royal Order....

Kitty, Kitty

Ohhh voluptuous, tender Woman
You activate the savage
Turn up the fire a few extra notches
Your presence is refreshing
Your loving is my latest and greatest inspiration
We come together naturally
We fit together so perfect
Beauty and the Savage
Heeere Kitty Kitty
I love my thick thicky
Juicy and tender
I will feed her wit' the daily recommended dose of the
Noble Diet
Keepin' her full until she purrs
Heeere Kitty Kitty
I love the way your skirt dances
As you strut down the Cat Walk
Hair flowing in the wind
With a smile that will light up the darkest room
My fe-fe, poo-poo
Mi Amor'
Who said it was too soon?

Timeless

I have prepared myself for your arrival my entire life
Woman, I am man in shining armor
Fearless and mighty where I stand
Certified and proven durable to protect you and love you
Who said it was too soon?
God has decided to bless us here and now
Just when I was beginning to believe it was only my
imagination
You appear so radiant
My Goddess
Whispering, "Julius, please be gentle."
The warmth of your soothing voice defrosts my soul
Who said it was too soon?
Our energy is too familiar to have ever been strangers
We found each other and made mad passionate love
Like two old lovers that have known each other for years
Muscles clench, clench, clench
Sweat drips drops, drip drops
From your nipple onto my tongue
Who said it was too soon for us to love like this?
Tomorrow is not promised
My God does not make mistakes…

The Unheard Voice

Drugs, guns, alcohol and prison…
I represent the unheard voice of many projects
The product from a series of governmental experiments
Experiments like, let's see what happens when you trap a
nigga
Give him Drugs, Guns, Alcohol and Prison
With daily images of fantasy transmitted into each
household
With constant soliciting from gigantic companies and their
products
Without any real opportunity to earn money
It's so easy to find
Drugs, Guns, Alcohol and Prison
I want to escape
Move my babies away
It seems there is nowhere safe
Teachers won't teach us because they don't get paid
enough
To care about us or our future
So it's Drugs, Guns, Alcohol and Prison
My city is infested with drugs to escape depression
I can't afford to pay attention to the voice of reason
When my utilities are disconnected
My tank running on empty
I vow to get rich or die trying
Drugs, Guns, Alcohol and Prison
Has become so alluring
So seductive
As I'm pursuing love and happiness on these cold streets

Off I go, unleashed and starving
Chasing after this American dollar
In my black Dickies, black Jordans, black Detroit-fitted cap

Burner off safety
William Lynch made me
Drugs, Guns, Alcohol and Prison…

Who's That Nigga?

Who's that nigga that talks loud
Masquerading around town like a Boss
Grinning from ear to ear spending money at the bars
Who's that nigga?
With the tough talk but knows not how to walk the walk
Selling dreams to the young and neglected
Gangster star stricken, tender Black Queen in need of a
King
He has fallen unto the hands of you
Drunken, disgusting, undetermined coward without a plan
He has created a family and abandoned them
Leaving the Queen of elegance with bitterness and several
mannish bastard children in need of their Father
Who is that Nigga?
For it is not just one alone
The Niggaz know who they are
Become a man Nigga
A man who takes care of home…

Don't Waste It

Time is too precious to be wasted
You can never get it back
You will regret getting knocked up because you thought
you were in love
Snap out of it
I know the ghetto can be depressing but it's really how you
look at it and
what you make of it
Half full or half empty,
The choice is yours
To be a leader or a follower
You may look delicious right now but you are not getting
any younger
The decision is yours to honor your temple
Baby girl, do you know where you are going to?
Do you like the things that life is showing you?
Where are you going?
Your baby will look at you and follow in your footsteps
You will regret bringing a child into poverty, unwedded
and fatherless
Time is too precious to be wasted
Learn how to earn…
Find out who you are first

Phenomenon

In 1716, William Lynch gathered all the slave masters and gave a lecture. The Making of a Slave. In his speech he gave a blueprint on how to make and break a slave. At the end of his speech he said it would take some sort of Phenomenon to undo his theory which has lasted over five centuries. In 2008 we were elected our first Black President, Barack Hussein Obama. He is that phenomenon...

Researching and learning America's history
Understanding with clarity
The beginning of the original man
The origin of field negroes versus house negroes
Black heritage and the revolution
The underground railroad and Huey P Newton
Benjamin Banneker and his strategic planning
This is our history
A new day is upon us with new leadership
America ain't neva' seen nothin' like this
November 4th, 2008 we made history
The little engine that could, finally did
Yes we can, do, and will!!!!!
Your American spirit is so refreshing
Your beautiful family exemplifies Black love and unity
Congratulations President Barack Obama
Thank you for reactivating hope in the Negro spirit
America ain't neva' seen nothing like this...

God's Blessing

No one stood with me
All forsook me, even left me for dead or to crack up into
little pieces
My God stands with me
He has strengthened me
So that His message could be delivered through me
I 'm the prime example of unwavering faith
My seat is reserved in God's heavenly kingdom
All glory unto him
Forever and ever, a man is born
Vengeance is mine said the Lord I serve
Those who live by the sword, shall die by the sword
These words I'm spittin' were written
Now being heard for all to listen
All His children who can hear it
Know that when friends and family fail
He won't
The most benevolent and merciful
God's Blessing…

Professor Julius Noble is a poet, writer, community advocate and emcee. He is signed to the *Noble Trinity Music* label as a hip-hop artist and poet. He is among the distinguished poets and authors published by *Glover Lane Press*. A proud Detroit native, Professor Noble splits his time between the West and East Coast working on his forthcoming rap album and working on his second and third books. For more information about Professor Noble's live performances and book tour, visit www.nobletrinitymusiclabel.com You may email Professor Noble your thoughts about this book or inquire about a live performance at pjnoble912@gmail.com

EXPLOSIVE EARGASMS (Glover Lane Press) is a collection of poetry and spoken word by Professor Julius Noble chronicling his journey of birth to manhood. From the gritty streets of Detroit, Michigan to his creative and spiritual rebirth in California, Professor Noble exposes the pain, realizations, awakenings of growing up in Motor City and his rise to fame as a poet and hip-hop artist on the Noble Trinity Music label.

"Explosive Eargasms is a literary uprising."
B-GLAM Book Club

"Professor Noble's debut book opens every door and window and leaves no stone unturned." Urban Post Book Reviews

"Explosive Eargasms represents a rare and important voice in the literary market."
Your World Media

EXPLOSIVE EARGASMS CD

IF YOU DID NOT PURCHASE THE CD WITH THE BOOK, YOU MAY PURCHASE IT NOW @ WWW.NOBLETRINITYMUSICLABEL.COM

www.ingramcontent.com/pod-product-compliance
Lightning Source LLC
Chambersburg PA
CBHW071457070426
42452CB00040B/1859